"I have known Danny for many years, and not only value his friendship, but admire his amazing zeal for the lost. May God continue to bless him and bless this important book."

—Ray Comfort,
author and evangelist

"Danny Lehmann is one of my favorite creative thinkers and Bible-lovers. He is gifted in making things about God and His Word very simple and understandable. *Is the Holy Bible Wholly True?* is a book that does exactly that! Danny tackles some of the hardest questions people ask about the Bible with solid, accurate, and inspirational answers, giving evidence of the God who really exists and who has communicated His love and His message for mankind through the inspired and authoritative Scriptures. I believe your heart and your mind will be encouraged as you read this book about the greatest book of all time, the Bible."

—Darlene Cunningham,
co-founder of
Youth With A Mission

"Danny has been a friend and mentor to me, our pastors, and many of those in our church. He brings application to God's Word as only a few can do. I highly recommend his new book *Is the Holy Bible Wholly True?* for your spiritual growth and encouragement."

—Pastor Bill Stonebraker,
Calvary Chapel Honolulu

IS THE HOLY BIBLE WHOLLY TRUE?

IS THE HOLY BIBLE WHOLLY TRUE?

DANNY LEHMANN

YWAM Publishing
P.O. Box 55787 • Seattle, WA 98155 • 425-771-1153
ywampublishing.com

YWAM Publishing is the publishing ministry of Youth With A Mission (YWAM), an international missionary organization of Christians from many denominations dedicated to presenting Jesus Christ to this generation. To this end, YWAM has focused its efforts in three main areas: (1) training and equipping believers for their part in fulfilling the Great Commission (Matthew 28:19), (2) personal evangelism, and (3) mercy ministry (medical and relief work).

To learn more about our books and materials, call (425) 771-1153 or (800) 922-2143 or email books@ywampublishing.com. Visit us online at www.ywampublishing.com.

Is the Holy Bible Wholly True?

Published by YWAM Publishing
a ministry of Youth With A Mission
P.O. Box 55787, Seattle, WA 98155-0787

ISBN 978-164836-160-9 (hardcover)

First printing 2025

Printed in the United States of America

CONTENTS

INTRODUCTION

The Greatest Book of All Time

No book in human history compares to the Bible. It is the best-selling (five billion copies), most translated (with portions in more than 3,700 languages), and most influential book of all time.

The Bible is formed from a small library of sixty-six books of both human and divine origin, all of which point us to Jesus. Forty different authors from a variety of backgrounds contributed to it over a 1,500-year period. Their work covers hundreds of controversial subjects and includes various literary forms: stories, poetry, biographies, legal documents, riddles, letters, testimonies, prophesy, and apocalyptic literature.

The Bible has influenced kings and paupers, transformed nations, and changed untold billions of lives, including mine. Yet for all that, there are billions more who remain convinced that the Bible is just another magical and mythical book that sits atop the crowded list of religious literature. Even some who seem to revere the Bible treat it as nothing more than a "hunt and peck" spiritual guidance system.

My attempt in this little volume is to persuade you, dear reader, to consider my proposition that the Bible is indeed "holy and wholly true" because its Author is holy and true and because its contents match up with reality. First, I allow the Bible to speak for itself, and I highlight some of the many benefits to an individual or a nation committed to obeying its precepts. Second, I present compelling evidence from external sources that the Bible is not just one more religious book but is trustworthy in all that it affirms. Scholars throughout the centuries affirm it as a combination of accurate history, scientific facts, and time-tested wisdom.

At this point I must acknowledge that there have indeed been people who have misused the Bible for their own ends. Muslims bring up the Crusades as an example of such abuse. Others note that many "Christians" have used passages in the Bible to justify slavery, racism, violence, anti-Semitism, and other injustices. My female friends could rightly object to the church using Bible verses out of context to push women to the margins of church life. All of this ugliness results from a misunderstanding, misapplication, or twisting of Scripture.

While the Bible at times has been used in very unbiblical ways, it still deserves recognition as the most helpful and influential book in human history. The evidence of history is that wherever the straightforward teaching of the Bible has been rightly applied and obeyed, society has undergone a moral and spiritual revolution.

SHIMABUKU: A TRANSFORMED COMMUNITY

When American troops captured the island of Okinawa toward the end of World War II, they found it in appalling social and moral condition. Then they reached the village of Shimabuku, where they were greeted by two old men, one of them carrying a Bible.

War correspondent Clarence Hall, who reported the story for *Reader's Digest* magazine, described how the Americans entered the village cautiously, suspicious of a trap, only to find it spotlessly clean, its fields tilled and fertile and everything a model of order and good stewardship, in stark contrast to surrounding villages. The reason? Some thirty years earlier, an American missionary had visited Shimabuku. He had stayed only long enough to make two converts (those two old men), teach them some hymns, and leave them a Japanese translation of the Bible. Guided by the Bible, those men had transformed their community. Shimabuku had no jail or brothel, no drunkenness or divorce. Instead, the people lived healthy, happy, and fulfilled lives. Shimabuku was an oasis of love and purity in a desert of degradation.

Clarence Hall summed up his feelings in the words of his astonished driver. "Maybe we're using the wrong kind of weapons to change the world."[1]

FAITH AND LOVE

What happened in Shimabuku is a testimony to the power of the Bible to radically change both individual lives and whole cities. Like the two old men, you can participate with God in this transformation.

One thing I learned early in my Christian walk is that, while my worldview is supported by the Bible and the witness of others, it requires regular steps of faith. As Hebrews 11:6 says, "And without faith it is impossible to please God, because anyone who comes to him must believe that he exists and that he rewards those who earnestly seek him."

Faith illuminates the written Word of God and helps to guide us through life's twists and turns. When evangelist Billy Graham and other great Christian leaders accepted by faith that the Bible is wholly true, God used them to do great things. And He will do great things through you if you take steps of faith.

The great things to which I'm referring include not only preaching the gospel, but also feeding the hungry, healing the sick and oppressed, and ministering to the brokenhearted. Jesus cares. Yes, He cares about our spiritual life, but He also cares about our physical bodies and the interactions we have with others. Loving Jesus will prompt you to do all these things and more.

CHAPTER 1

Did God Write Stuff Down?

"It is a basic tenet of the Christian faith that we believe what we believe not because human beings have invented it, but because God has revealed it."

—John Stott, *I Believe in Preaching*

As my scholarly friend David J. Hamilton has said, the Bible is God's love letter to humanity. "Within the first few verses of the Bible these words are found: 'And God said…' (Gen. 1:3). This and two thousand similar statements in the Scriptures confirm that our God is a communicator *par excellence*. His desire to speak to us forms the very essence of the Bible."[1]

Yes, the God of the Bible is a God who speaks, and He is still speaking today to those who follow Him. In the Bible's opening pages, which describe the creation of the world, we see God engaging His newly created beings in conversation. As the relationship develops, the Lord speaks to them in various ways. And even when the first humans disobey Him, God continues to pursue them. The Bible is a record of this divine-human connection, and throughout its pages are stories, laws, and teachings that show us the way to a life-giving, holy relationship with God.

So when I ask the question "Is the Holy Bible wholly true?" my answer is that the Holy Bible is indeed wholly true.

The skeptical reader might accuse me of circular reasoning, that is, that I am quoting the Bible to prove the Bible. To which I respond, "Guilty as charged." But if you read on with an open heart and mind, you will discover other evidence. Multiple sources outside the Bible, when examined honestly, give the skeptic ample reason to give, as I have, a resounding "YES" to the question at hand.

A TALE OF TWO PREACHERS

One of the greatest stories I've ever read about how this question was answered with honest conviction and consequences is that of two Youth for Christ evangelists named Charles Templeton and Billy Graham.

Templeton founded a church that soon overflowed its 1,200-seat sanctuary. He and Billy Graham grew in friendship with each other. But soon doubts began to nag at Templeton, particularly the issue of how a God of love could allow evil and suffering to exist. Eventually these challenges caused Templeton to renounce the Christian faith. He later wrote a book called *Farewell to God: My Reasons for Rejecting the Christian Faith*. He went on to pursue a career in journalism and writing. His friend Billy Graham went on to become…well… Billy Graham!

For decades Billy remained one of the most admired men in the world, having touched the lives of millions of people. Both Templeton and Graham went through what we might call a crisis of faith, despite "many convincing proofs" (Acts 1:3) and compelling evidence in support of the Bible's integrity. Both needed to take what Søren Kierkegaard famously called a "leap of faith" and accept not only Jesus, but the Bible as God's Word. Indeed, we all need to take such a leap.

While Templeton was busy researching reasons for rejecting the Christian faith, Billy hiked into the San Bernardino Mountains of California and, sitting on a tree stump, he gripped his Bible, dropped to his knees, and confessed he was going to, by faith, accept the Holy Bible as wholly true.

I love the iconic image of Billy as a young preacher from North Carolina leaning over a pulpit, holding a Bible, pointing a finger to the sky, and pronouncing, "The Bible says…"

The book you're holding is my attempt to give you good reason to affirm the Bible as a strong foundation for your life. I challenge you to take a leap of faith. Consider not only what the Bible says about itself but what can be "proven" by an honest examination of eyewitness testimony along with archaeological, historical, prophetic, scientific, and explanatory evidence that authenticates claims found in Scripture.

Back to Charles Templeton: In Lee Strobel's excellent book *The Case for Faith*, he describes his interview with an elderly Templeton.[2] Even an accomplished scholar like Strobel could not shake the older gentleman from his skepticism regarding the Bible. Templeton told Strobel that while he maintained an admiration for Billy Graham, he just couldn't bring himself to faith and opined that Billy had committed intellectual suicide.

At this point in the conversation, Strobel felt compelled to steer the conversation away from controversial issues and focus instead on Jesus Himself. Templeton's voice took on more of a melancholy and reflective tone. He spoke of Jesus with great admiration. His voice began to crack. "I…miss…Him!" he said.

Strobel was dumbfounded and mused to himself, "Was this an unguarded glimpse into Templeton's soul? What did he mean that he 'missed Jesus' and why did this erupt in such a guttural emotional response?" Strobel left the interview not knowing exactly what had happened, but he realized that forty-plus years of unbelief still had not cracked the love Templeton experienced from Jesus.

The theologically minded among us might wonder about the salvation of a man who spent three decades preaching the gospel and the next thirty-plus years denouncing the God of the Bible. Are we "once saved, always saved" and "eternally secure" once we have accepted Christ, or did Templeton lose his salvation when he turned from Christ? Scholars still argue over this question. But it does bring out an essential point as we approach the Bible. While the Bible does give us rational and intellectual foundations for faith in Christ, we must also have our own personal encounter with a God who reveals Himself to us as we ask Him and even sometimes when we don't!

The rest of this book will present the rational side of the Christian faith, but we must never leave out the role of the Holy Spirit in convicting people of sin and drawing them to Christ (John 6:44). Reason and Revelation have joined together, and what God has joined together let us not separate!

DID GOD REALLY SAY THAT?

Do you know what the first question recorded in the Bible is? The questioner is the crafty old serpent in the garden! He says to the woman, "Did God really say, 'You must not eat from any tree in the garden'?" (Gen. 3:1).

As we follow the narrative, the woman says to the serpent, "We may eat fruit from the trees in the garden, but God did say, 'You must not eat fruit from the tree that is in the middle of the garden, and you must not touch it, or you will die.'" The serpent responds, "You will not certainly die. For God knows that when you eat from it your eyes will be opened, and you will be like God, knowing good and evil" (Gen. 3:2–5). The Tempter was trying to get the first couple to doubt that God said what He meant and meant what He said! In other words, the satanic temptation was "God didn't really say what you think He said."

This tree was not simply the tree of good and evil, it was the tree of the *knowledge* of good and evil and thereby an avenue to become like God. When the serpent held out the forbidden fruit, he was in essence offering them their own individual "godhood." This offer to become our own god is a theme of other religions, such as Hinduism, Buddhism, and Mormonism. Ever since the Fall of humanity—ever since Adam and Eve—how has it worked out to have men and women acting as gods, determining for themselves what is good and evil? Not very well.

As you peruse the content of this book, I encourage you to consider, in light of the evidence, that God has indeed spoken to us through His Word, the Bible, and that unlike Adam and Eve, we have the opportunity to say yes to the question, "Did God really say that?"—and yes to the question, "Is the Holy Bible wholly true?"

If you are a Christian, you will be strengthened in your faith that God indeed has spoken. If you are not, I pray that this book will help you to consider not only the whole Bible, but especially the content about Jesus Christ and the salvation He offers you.

The first question in the Bible, in the words of British scholar and author C. S. Lewis, led to a choice that "went terribly wrong" for the first couple. We, however, can make a different decision. As Billy Graham did in accepting the Bible by faith, I encourage you to follow his lead and accept the evidence that the Holy Bible is wholly true.

CHAPTER 2

The "Useful" Bible

"Christians feed on scripture. It nurtures the soul as food nurtures the body. Christians don't just learn or use scripture, we take it into our lives in such a way that it gets metabolized into acts of love, cups of cold water and missions into all the world."

—Eugene Peterson, *Eat This Book*

It says in 2 Timothy 3:16, "All Scripture is God-breathed and is useful." Let's not miss the two amazing adjectives Paul uses to describe the very nature of Scripture. It is, first of all, "God-breathed"—from two Greek words fused together, *Theos* (God) and *pneustos* (breath or spirit). Allow this to blow your mind for a minute!

Words that originate in God's mind, He exhales onto the pages of Scripture! His breath gives the biblical words their spiritual power. As Jesus said, "The words I have spoken to you—they are full of the Spirit and life" (John 6:63). The words *breath* and *spirit* are often used interchangeably in the Bible. For instance, when Jesus met with His disciples, He "breathed on them and said, 'Receive the Holy Spirit'" (John 20:22), and Ezekiel prophesied for the Lord in the valley of dry bones, "I will make breath enter you, and you will come to life.... I will put my Spirit in you and you will live" (Ezek. 37:5, 14).

This brings us to the other adjective given to the Word of God—that it is "useful." In some English versions the word *ophelimos* is translated "profitable" or "beneficial." God wants us to profit or benefit from our interaction with Scripture. The Bible is not just some feel-good devotional meant to give us a religious pick-me-up when we're bummed out. Its primary "use" is that we "may be thoroughly equipped for every good work" (2 Tim. 3:17).

In the previous chapter, we learned that God speaks and that He is still speaking to us today. Because one of the foundational ways He makes Himself known to us is through His Word, the Holy Scriptures, we need to place the utmost importance on them. In them, God reveals who He is, who we are, and how we relate to Him and His purposes for His creation! If we want to know the truth about God, humanity, and the world, God reveals all of this in Scripture.

We pay careful attention to Scripture because it is the record of God's rescue of humanity. Remember the choice that went terribly wrong for the first couple? We and everything in creation are broken by sin. From beginning to end, the Bible is a faithful witness to God's work to reconcile all things to Himself—including each of us (Col. 1:20–22; 2 Cor. 5:18–21).

All of Scripture points us to Jesus. In the Old Testament, about seven hundred years before the birth of Jesus, the prophet Isaiah wrote, "But he was pierced for our transgressions, he was crushed for our iniquities; the punishment that brought us peace was on him, and by his wounds we are healed" (Isa. 53:5). Hundreds of years later, after having the astounding privilege of personally knowing and being a disciple of the promised Messiah, the apostle Peter preached, "All the prophets testify about him that everyone who believes in him receives forgiveness of sins through his name" (Acts 10:43). Sprinkled throughout the Gospels and the letters circulated by the early church are countless "gospel in a nutshell" jewels. Don't miss them. (See Rom. 5:8; 1 John 4:10; 1 Pet. 3:18; Col. 1:13–23; 1 Cor. 15:1–6; Gal. 1:1–5; John 1:1–18; John 3:16; better yet, read it all!) The apostle Paul explains, "Faith comes from hearing the message, and the message is heard through the word about Christ" (Rom. 10:17).

Not only is the Bible a faithful guide to our salvation in Christ, but it is also indispensable in every part of our lives as followers of Jesus. Paul, knowing he was soon to be martyred (2 Tim. 4:6), urged Timothy to reflect on the spiritual parenting he had received from his mom and grandma (2 Tim. 1:5) as well as all he had learned from Paul himself and to make "use" of the sacred Scriptures in four areas:

1. TEACHING: LEARNING WHAT IS RIGHT

A disciple is a learner, and for a disciple there is no higher priority than learning and obeying the Word. Earlier Paul told Timothy to "immerse" himself in the Scriptures (1 Tim. 4:15 ESV). He instructed him, "Keep a close watch on yourself and on the teaching. Persist in this, for by so doing you will save both yourself and your hearers" (1 Tim. 4:16 ESV). The word that is translated "the teaching" in this verse is *didaskalia.* It is used nineteen times by Paul, mostly in his letters to young church leaders Timothy and Titus. Some translations render it "doctrine." Paul consistently challenges Timothy and Titus to adhere to and teach "sound doctrine" (1 Tim. 1:10, 4:6, Titus 2:1, 7, 10) as well as to warn their members against false teachers (1 Tim. 4:1–4). Jesus himself predicted false prophets and false teachers would arise and deceive many (Matt. 24:4–5, 11, 24). Hence, the need for developing a passionate hunger for the truth.

When the church was born on the day of Pentecost, these new believers "devoted themselves to the apostles' teaching" (Acts 2:42). Later, Paul warned of people who would "abandon the faith" (1 Tim. 4:1) while Jude spoke of "the faith that was once for all entrusted to God's holy people" (Jude 3). There was a body of objective truth called "the faith" that was agreed upon by the apostles and early church fathers that needed to be taught to both build up the church and protect the flock from false teachers. This body of "good doctrine" (1 Tim. 4:6 ESV) later developed into the "canon" of Holy Scripture and into the various church creeds. More on this in chapter 8.

2. REPROVING: LEARNING WHAT IS NOT RIGHT

"The ear that listens to life-giving reproof will dwell among the wise" (Prov. 15:31 ESV).

Several Bible passages teach us the value of a loving rebuke. Here are just two examples: "Do not harbor hatred against your brother. Rebuke your neighbor directly, and you will not incur guilt because of him" (Lev. 19:17 CSB). "If thy brother trespass against thee, rebuke him; and if he repent, forgive him" (Luke 17:3 KJV).

We see in the second verse above that there are two people involved in the rebuke: the person who is giving the rebuke and the person who is receiving it. Those giving the rebuke should be careful to ensure their reproof is "life-giving" (Prov. 15:31 ESV) and always have restoration as their goal. As Paul taught members of the early church, "If someone is caught in a sin, you who live by the Spirit should restore that person gently" (Gal. 6:1). Nathan the prophet was commissioned by God to correct David regarding his affair with Bathsheba. Nathan is a good example of how to deliver a corrective word. He even used a word picture to assist him in giving his rebuke a safe landing (see 2 Sam. 12).

On the other hand, the person who is on the receiving end of a rebuke should maintain a humble and teachable spirit to hear what the Lord may be speaking through the person doing the correcting. Jesus spoke several times of having "ears to hear" (e.g., Rev. 2-3 KJV).

The word *rebuke* means "to reprimand by exposing a wrong." It's one thing to get into the Word. It is quite another to get the Word into us, sometimes through the biblical delivery device of a good old-fashioned rebuke.

3. CORRECTING: LEARNING HOW TO GET RIGHT

"Corrective discipline is the way to life" (Prov. 6:23 CSB).

"Houston, we have a problem." These words have become a part of American slang ever since Apollo 13 suffered so many malfunctions on April 13, 1970, that there was a real potential for Commander James Lovell and his crew to be quite literally lost in space. Millions watched as Mission Control and the spaceship engineered a "course correction."

"Whoever hates correction is stupid," Proverbs 12:1 says. It seems at first glance that rebuking and correcting are synonymous, but there is quite a difference. A rebuke is a verbal smackdown, an initial slap in the face to get someone's attention and to warn them that they're heading in the wrong direction. Correction as used in the Bible here has to do with a process of using Scripture to turn someone away from sure peril and make a course correction that sets them up for what author and pastor Eugene Peterson has called "a long obedience in the same direction."

There is an overstatement often made by those of us involved in evangelism: "Christianity is not a list of dos and don'ts but a personal relationship with God." This is only partly true, however, as there are hundreds of dos and don'ts in the Bible. This is why we need to allow the Scriptures to correct us when we are going in the wrong direction as well as inspire us to go in the right one.

4. TRAINING: LEARNING TO STAY RIGHT

Jesus calls us to learn from Him (Matt. 11:29). A disciple is a disciplined learner. Paul told Timothy to "discipline yourself for the purpose of godliness" (1 Tim. 4:7 NASB). The word *gymnazo* translated here as "discipline" is taken from the Greco-Roman world of athletic competition. Timothy, being a young leader, is exhorted here to discipline himself much like the athlete in the gym.

Elsewhere Paul expands on this idea with a running metaphor: "Do you not know that in a race all the runners run, but only one gets the prize? Run in such a way as to get the prize. Everyone who competes in the games goes into strict training. They do it to get a crown that will not last, but we do it to get a crown that will last forever" (1 Cor. 9:24–25). While athletes set their sights on a physical prize, our goal is to achieve a spiritual prize. Paul said of himself, "I press on toward the goal to win the prize for which God has called me heavenward in Christ Jesus" (Phil. 3:14). As for athletes, reaching our goal requires "strict training" (1 Cor. 9:25).

As with the terms *rebuke* and *correct*, the words *teaching* and *training* must be distinguished from each other. *Teaching* simply refers to the transfer of information from one person to another, whereas *training* has to do with on-the-job experience or "apprenticeship."

Ultimately, Paul's goal for Timothy was much like Jesus's goal for His disciples: that the disciple should be as his teacher. Two epic books on the subject, *The Master Plan of Evangelism* (Robert Coleman) and *The Training of the Twelve* (A. B. Bruce) point out that, contrary to popular belief, Jesus did not spend most of his time with the crowds but primarily invested his time training the twelve. In other words, Jesus did what he tells us to do: "Make disciples" (Matt. 28:19).

Likewise, Paul followed Jesus's example and spent much time with Timothy, Titus, and more than forty other people he mentions in his letters by name. He wrote to Timothy, "The things you have heard me say in the presence of many witnesses entrust to reliable people who will also be qualified to teach others" (2 Tim. 2:2). Paul poured his life into Timothy, who was to pour into "reliable" people who would teach others.

We see from all the various Scripture passages in this chapter that the Bible is given to us for many important purposes. It is truly indispensable. Note that Scripture is not given to us to make us theology geeks. Nor is its truth to be used as a spiritual sword to dice and slice those who have different viewpoints—people we might think are less enlightened than we perceive ourselves to be, and therefore, we think, in dire need of our application of Scripture. Scripture is not our personal property to divide into topical beachheads by which we might drop our truth bombs.

Instead, remember all the legitimate purposes of Scripture we covered in this chapter: First, Jesus Himself says, "The words I have spoken to you—they are full of the Spirit and life" (John 6:63). And who can forget that, in Scripture, God reveals Himself and His plan for salvation? Scripture is also given to us so that we "may be thoroughly equipped for every good work" (2 Tim. 3:17). We are to allow the Scriptures to correct us when we are going in the wrong direction as well as inspire us to go in the right one. Scripture shows us how to be a disciple and how to make disciples.

God says, "Here is my Word—use it!"

CHAPTER 3
Can I Get a Witness?
(Eyewitness Testimony)

"The Gospels were written within living memory of the events they recount. Mark's gospel was written well within the lifetime of the eyewitnesses, while the other three canonical Gospels were written in the period when living eyewitnesses were becoming scarce, exactly at the point in time when their testimony would perish with them were it not put in writing."

—Richard Bauckham, *Jesus and the Eyewitnesses*

Before I was a believer and while still in my teens, I was arrested and charged with the crime of "The Willful and Malicious Destruction of Property," which according to Maryland state law carried a penalty of up to three years in jail and/or a fine of up to $2,500. The guy whose car had been totaled swore he would prosecute me all the way to prison.

The fact that this was my third arrest in six months added to my fear that I was facing serious jail time. In fear and trembling I went to my father, who was an accomplished attorney in Baltimore, and asked for help.

I also recruited my brother Steve, who was home on leave from Vietnam. On the trial date I marched into the courtroom in a suit and tie, sporting my long blonde hair in a ponytail. Steve followed with his Marine Corps dress duds. Both he and Dad were to be my character witnesses.

The judge gave me a good tongue-lashing, then invited Dad and Steve back into his chambers. They had a drink together, and the judge told the two of them that he knew I was a good kid and just got involved with the wrong people, so he let me go with a slap on the wrist. This mercy was accompanied by a threat that if I appeared in his courtroom again, I better bring my toothbrush. To which I humbly said, "Thank you, Your Honor."

I exited the courtroom that day knowing that what saved my bacon was the fact that my accuser didn't show up to prosecute the case. If this eyewitness had testified that I had destroyed his car, I likely wouldn't have walked out of that courtroom a free man.

As in the United States, among most civilized societies, including ancient Israel, an eyewitness testimony is always the highest form of proof that an action has taken place or not. As Deuteronomy 19:15 says, "A matter must be established by the testimony of two or three witnesses."

J. Warner Wallace was a cold-case detective in the Los Angeles Police Department for more than twenty years.

In his examination of eyewitnesses, he would employ four "tests" to validate the truth they proclaimed:

1. *Presence* – Were they actually there? You can't be an eyewitness if you were not there to see the crime.

2. *Corroborating evidence* – Is there corroborating evidence in the form of other witnesses or circumstantial evidence?

3. *Firmness of testimony* – Has their testimony remained firm, or has it changed over time?

4. *Bias* – Do they possess a bias that would cause them to lie?

One of the remarkable things about the Bible is that it records lots of eyewitness testimony, from both authors of Bible narratives and other followers of Christ who claim to have seen Jesus alive after His crucifixion. These eyewitness testimonies were dubbed "many convincing proofs" by Luke in Acts 1:3.

THE BIBLE'S EYEWITNESSES

The Apostle Peter was an eyewitness. Here is some of his testimony:

"God has raised this Jesus to life, and we are all witnesses of it" (Acts 2:32).

"We are witnesses of this" (Acts 3:15).

"We cannot help speaking about what we have seen and heard" (Acts 4:20).

"We are witnesses of these things" (Acts 5:32).

"We are witnesses of everything he did" (Acts 10:39).

"He appeared to Cephas [Peter], and then to the Twelve" (1 Cor. 15:5).

"We did not follow cleverly devised stories when we told you about the coming of our Lord Jesus Christ in power, but we were eyewitnesses of his majesty" (2 Pet. 1:16).

Thomas was an eyewitness.

"Because you have seen me, you have believed; blessed are those who have not seen and yet have believed" (see John 20:24–30).

John was an eyewitness.

"That which was from the beginning, which we have heard, which we have seen with our eyes, which we have looked at and our hands have touched—this we proclaim concerning the Word of life. The life appeared; we have seen it and testify to it" (1 John1:1–2).

Luke drew his material from eyewitnesses.

"Many have undertaken to draw up an account of the things that have been fulfilled among us, just as they were handed down to us by those who from the first were eyewitnesses and servants of the word" (Luke 1:1–2).

Paul was an eyewitness.

Paul encountered the risen Lord on the road to Damascus (Acts 9:1–19). In his letters, Paul lists fourteen people by name who were eyewitnesses of the risen Christ—Paul himself, James, and the twelve apostles (1 Cor. 15:3–8).

Mary Magdalene was an eyewitness.
She and other women were the first to see the risen Jesus at the tomb on Easter morning (Matt. 28:1–10).

Matthias was an eyewitness.
As the disciple who replaced Judas, he fulfilled the condition of an eyewitness of the Resurrection (Acts 1:20–26).

The fact that all the apostles except John died a martyr's death must cause us to ask, "Why would they all be willing to die for a lie?"

Perhaps the most persuasive argument in favor of the Resurrection is Paul's declaration that, in addition to the above examples, Jesus appeared to more than five hundred people at the same time (1 Cor. 15:6). He said most of them were still alive when he wrote this letter (in AD 54), making his claim an unspoken invitation to check out the facts.

I have mused to myself that Paul quipped to the Corinthians, "Hey, I'm not making this stuff up! If you don't believe me, go track down some of these folks who are still alive and ask them what they saw that day."

Paul wrote 1 Corinthians about twenty years after the Crucifixion. If "most" of the 500 were still alive and "most" means more than 250, this adds to the list of eyewitnesses who could be corroborated. The only way these people saw Jesus was that He took the initiative to reveal Himself to them!

What an incredible God we serve! Not only did Thomas (who was martyred for his faith in India) have his faith lifted by seeing Jesus in that upper room, but the New Testament gives us hundreds of examples of eyewitnesses to His resurrection.

When we say today that we "witness" for Christ, we must keep in mind that no matter how dynamic and dramatic our conversion may have been, our witness to what Christ has done in our lives is secondary to those who saw the risen Christ. Someone has wisely said, "Christianity is a subjective relationship with God based on objective truth—the truth that Christ rose from the dead."

This brings us to an all-important point. No other religion is based on the testimony of eyewitnesses declaring that their risen founder had risen from the dead. No other religious leader ever made such a claim—or had more than 250 eyewitnesses backing up the story.

While having so many testify about seeing the risen Christ may not prove by mathematical calculation that the gospel is true, it does, however, give us pause to think about how significant these eyewitnesses were in launching this new faith called Christianity.

CHAPTER 4

Weltanschauung
(What It Is and Why It Matters)

"Worldview is any ideology, philosophy, theology, movement, or religion that provides an overarching approach to understanding God, the world, and man's relationship to God and the world."

—David Noebel, *The Battle for Truth*

On a speaking tour of the Netherlands a few years ago, I had a day off. So my wife, Linda, and I took a train from Amsterdam to Haarlem to visit The Hiding Place, made famous by Corrie ten Boom and her family, who hid Jews from the Nazis during World War II.

I was inspired by the ten Boom family as I heard the story of their great faith. When the tour was over, our guide said something that I will never forget: "Over fifty million people died because of the madness of one man!" On the train ride back to Amsterdam, those words stuck in my head—"Fifty million people died"—including all of Corrie's family.

Just after World War II, American scholar Richard M. Weaver published the book *Ideas Have Consequences.*

The Holocaust and all the evil that came out of World War II originated in the mind of one man and the way that man had learned to think about himself, Germany, and the rest of the world.

Adolph Hitler had a *Weltanschauung*—the German word for worldview or "world and life view"—that justified the killing of Jews and people of other races. A *Weltanschauung* is how one views or interprets reality. Some describe it as the lens through which we see the physical and spiritual world. What we Christians have in mind when saying we have a "biblical worldview" is that all of life is seen through biblical lenses. For instance, the reason we are "pro-life" regarding abortion is that the Bible teaches that all babies are made in the image of God and therefore have intrinsic value.

In 1925 Hitler wrote *Mein Kampf* (My Struggle) in which he outlined his racist worldview which grew into his extreme hatred for Jews, homosexuals, and other minorities. This was coupled with a belief in the extreme superiority of Germany's supposedly Aryan race.

Looking through these lenses, and drawing upon his extraordinary rhetorical and organizational skills, Hitler projected a vision to the German people: *We will rise from the ashes of World War I. Things will be messy for a while, but ultimately the Third Reich will triumph, and the world will be a better place.* Many German people caught his optimism, and the rest of the world paid the price.

Back to Corrie ten Boom. She was released from the Ravensbrück concentration camp on a technical error. After the war, Corrie traveled to more than sixty-five countries, using Bible passages, pithy illustrations, and quotable quotes to preach forgiveness. In one of her speaking engagements, she gave a sermon on loving your enemies. Afterward, one of her former guards came forward to ask her forgiveness for his cruel treatment of her. Although she struggled for a bit, she shook the man's hand and forgave him.

So, you may ask, what does this have to do with *Weltanschauung*? Much, in every way. I have chosen these two historical examples to illustrate that ideas do have consequences and influence how we think and act. Adolf Hitler and Corrie ten Boom had ideas that led to their polar-opposite *Weltanschauungs* and illustrate where I am going in this chapter. One worldview meant that Jews were a "problem" that needed a "final solution" (The Holocaust). The other worldview caused a woman to lay down her life to save some of those same Jews.

In her teaching on "The Belief Tree,"[1] Youth With A Mission cofounder Darlene Cunningham illustrates this in a word picture that is easy to understand. Our actions and decisions (the fruit on the tree) are determined by our values (the trunk). Our values are determined by our beliefs (the roots) and our beliefs are rooted in our worldview (the soil). See also Matthew 7:15–20.

Jesus calls His disciples to be the "salt of the earth" (Matt. 5:13), which presupposes that the salt is to be "in" and not only "of" the earth. Salt in ancient times was used not only to season food and bring out its flavor, but also to create thirst and act as a preservative against corruption. Jesus also calls His disciples "the light of the world" (Matt. 5:14). He says, "Let your light shine before others, that they may see your good deeds and glorify your Father in heaven" (Matt. 5:16). Most Christians throughout history have interpreted Jesus's words on the light of the world to refer to evangelism and the salt of the earth to refer to the influence that the church is to have in the world.

To have a biblical worldview simply means we align all of life with the teachings and model of Jesus. Abraham Kuyper, former prime minister of the Netherlands, said, "There is not a square inch in the whole domain of our human existence over which Christ, who is Sovereign over all, does not cry: 'Mine!'"

THE TWO-HANDED GOSPEL

Since the birth of the Christian church, well-meaning disciples of Christ have sought to interpret and apply these two biblical word pictures (of salt and light) as well as Jesus's two great commandments (to love God and our neighbor). For instance, if we have a biblical worldview, should we not lobby on the political front for pro-life legislation because we care about all babies, including non-Christian babies? Weren't Christian evangelists like Charles Finney and Christian legislators like William Wilberforce obeying God when they labored to stop the slave trade? William and Catherine Booth founded the Salvation Army because their worldview led them to see the world as a battlefield in which we are soldiers fighting forces of evil like drunkenness, sexual abuse, greed, and thievery.

My friend Don Stephens, director of Mercy Ships, coined the phrase "the Two-Handed Gospel" to describe our dual responsibility to evangelize the lost and care for the poor and marginalized.

Theologian John Stott put it this way:

> We serve. And in this we have (or should have) no ulterior motive. True, the gospel lacks visibility if we merely preach it, and lacks credibility if we who preach it are interested only in souls and have no concern about the welfare of people's bodies, situations, and communities. Yet the reason for our acceptance of social responsibility is not primarily in order to give the gospel either a visibility or a credibility it would otherwise lack, but rather simple uncomplicated compassion.[2]

The point is that we have a biblical responsibility to love our friends and neighbors and to show compassion to suffering people we don't know. In doing so we demonstrate that our God cares about their hurting bodies as well as their souls.

All of us have a soul and a body, and we have both physical and spiritual needs. God gave us His Word so we would know how we could fulfill those needs and the purpose for which we were created. Sometime in eternity past, the triune God said, "I think I'll make a Danny (substitute your name)." For some reason He made me five feet six rather than six feet five. As I look in the rearview mirror of my life, I am so grateful to have experienced fifty years of relationship with God and others, thousands of blessings, answers to prayer, and much more. God has given me a heart to love Him, a will to obey Him, a mind to understand Him, and a body with which to serve Him. I have been blessed by God's grace to take this "Two-Handed Gospel" to others.

ALL SPIRITUAL WORLDVIEWS CAN'T BE TRUE

Theologian Norman Geisler summarized and defined the various *Weltanschauungs* available to us:

> *Theism:* An infinite personal God exists beyond and in the universe.
>
> *Deism:* God created the world but is not in it. He wound it up and let it go.
>
> *Atheism:* No God exists beyond or in the universe.
>
> *Pantheism:* God is the universe, and everything is God.

Polytheism: Many finite gods exist beyond the world and in it.

Open theism: God is infinite and personal and dwells in time as we do.

All these worldviews cannot be right. One of them is. The Bible gives us sufficient evidence that there exists a good, infinite, personal, and loving God who wows us with His creation and woos us with His love and invites us into a dynamic relationship with Himself.

In my book *Clues: How Can We Know We Know?* I attempt to give compelling reasons why the Christian faith is true and show that Jesus Christ and His gospel are the means God has provided for salvation. I use courtroom imagery revolving around the biblical definition of faith. Hebrews 11:1 says, "Faith is the substance of things hoped for, *the evidence of things not seen*" (KJV, emphasis mine).

I acknowledge I can't prove the Bible is true like I can prove two plus two equals four, but I can give several "clues" that present a "preponderance of evidence." These clues would at least make a thinking person or skeptic consider the evidence upon which they could base their faith.

Is the Holy Bible Wholly True? is my attempt to reinforce the evidence I put forth in *Clues* and to offer a sequel focusing on the Bible. As with *Clues,* however, my objective is not to give an exhaustive treatment of the subject but to provide some basics on why hundreds of millions of people throughout history have chosen to trust the Bible to answer the big questions of life.

We will be looking at archaeology, predictive prophecy, manuscript evidence, and historical accuracy to give you a foundation upon which to build your faith. While being intellectually persuaded that the Bible is reliable is not a substitute for faith, it is a compelling path to a personal encounter with the God of the Bible. This evidence, if approached with a humble and teachable spirit, will change your life.

CHAPTER 5

Can You Dig It? (Archaeology)

"No archaeological discovery has ever controverted a biblical reference."

—Nelson Glueck, *Rivers in the Desert*

Archaeology may be defined as the study of the ancient and recent human past through material remains. Or we could simply say archaeologists dig up stuff left behind by our ancestors. Archaeologist Stuart Piggott called it the "science of rubbish." Archaeologists painstakingly sift through heaps of crumbling refuse, ancient shards of pottery, shattered buildings, and fragmented documents. Most are incredibly patient and detailed people who observe, search, discover, record, and preserve the buried remains of antiquity and use them to help reconstruct the lives of those who lived in ancient times.

Archaeology, however, is not an exact science as most remains are fragments and don't have a date stamped on them! An archaeologist's work leans heavily on other disciplines such as linguistics, history, numismatics (the study of coins), and so forth.

For instance, Luke, who wrote 27 percent of the New Testament (Luke and Acts), was the target of a skeptical archaeologist named Sir William Mitchell Ramsay, who set out to disprove the historical reliability of Luke's New Testament accounts. To his surprise, Ramsay not only verified over eighty historical details found in Acts alone but was converted to Christ!

Renowned Jewish archaeologist Rabbi Nelson Glueck famously said, "No archaeological discovery has ever controverted a biblical reference." Apologist Hank Hanegraaff quipped, "Truly with every turn of the archaeologist's spade, we continue to see evidence for the trustworthiness of Scripture."[1]

Archaeology as a discipline had its beginnings in 1846 when an Assyrian obelisk was discovered in what today is northern Iraq. The obelisk referred to Jehu, a Hebrew king from the ninth century BC (2 Chron. 22:7–9). For the first time, an archaeological find corroborated details from the Bible, and biblical archaeology was born. Since then, hundreds of archaeological discoveries have backed up the Scriptures.

For example, in 1961 an inscription was found near Jerusalem bearing the name "Pilate." It was the earliest known reference to this Roman governor outside the New Testament. In 1968, a first-century home in Capernaum was identified as that of the apostle Peter. In 1990, an ossuary (a box in which bones were buried) was found bearing the inscription and bones of

Caiaphas, the high priest who infamously pushed for Jesus's execution. In 1993, the first of many inscriptions mentioning the "House of David" was discovered.

Numerous other discoveries affirm the historical accuracy of the biblical narratives:

SODOM

Genesis 19 tells the story of God's judgment and fiery destruction of the city of Sodom. In October 2021, *Nature Scientific Reports* described an archaeological dig near the Dead Sea that revealed the cataclysmic destruction of a Middle Bronze Age city believed to be Sodom. Archaeologist Dr. Steven Collins began excavating the site in 2006, and when his team got down to the level dated circa 1650 BC, they uncovered a five-foot layer of soot with randomly scattered bits of melted brick and burnt fragments of human bones. They also discovered a shard of a jar with a strange glassy green glaze. Collins estimated that the heat technology to produce such a glaze would not exist for another twenty-four centuries.

JERICHO

Dr. John Garstang, director of the British School of Archaeology in Jerusalem, excavated the ruins of the biblical city of Jericho from 1929 to 1936. He found archaeological evidence that the city had been destroyed about 1400 BC, coinciding with the estimated date of the Joshua 6 report, which says, "The wall fell down flat." Dr. Garstang found that the wall had fallen. The thirty-foot wall was double, set about fifteen feet apart. The archaeologist found that the outer wall fell outward down the hillside dragging the inner wall and houses with it. Because of this linkage, they "fell down flat" rather than crumbling.

Joshua 6:24 says that they burned the city with fire. This fact was confirmed by the great layers of charcoal and ash that Garstang's team found while studying the ruins. Houses along the outer wall suffered the least damage because of the way the wall fell. Those inside were burned.

HEZEKIAH'S TUNNEL

Another confirmation of a biblical story is that of Hezekiah, thirteenth king of Judah. As Hezekiah prepared for Sennacherib's invasion in 701 BC, his men worked to maintain an adequate water supply within Jerusalem's walls (2 Kings 20:20, 2 Chron. 32:2–5). The workers cut a conduit underground through the rock to channel water from the Gihon Spring outside Jerusalem to the Pool of Siloam inside the city, thus diverting it from flowing into the Brook Kidron. This channel, known as Hezekiah's Tunnel, runs a crooked course for about seventeen hundred feet. Its average height is six feet. One can visit and walk through it even today. An inscription found in 1880 describes the workers cutting through the rock beginning at both ends and meeting triumphantly at the midpoint as one pick struck another.

These are just a few of many examples. As Nelson Glueck has pointed out, archaeology is affirming what the Bible has told us for centuries.

CHAPTER 6
The Presence of the Future (Prophecy)

"One of the most powerful arguments for the literal fulfillment of prophecy relating to Christ's future coming is the fact that prophecy was literally fulfilled at his first coming."

—Thomas Ice, "The Literal Fulfillment of Bible Prophecy"

Among the world's religious writings, the Bible alone has hundreds of specific, detailed predictions about events over which the writer had no control, many of which have already come to pass. The Bible stands alone in being accurate in the predictions it contains. Scholar J. Barton Payne compiled an epic *Encyclopedia of Biblical Prophecy.* He cites 1,817 predictions, 1,239 in the Old Testament and 578 in the New. For instance, the Bible predicts that the Messiah was to be

- born in Bethlehem (Micah 5:2)
- born to a virgin (Isa. 7:14)
- rejected by his own people (Ps. 118:22)

- betrayed by a friend (Ps. 41:9, John 13:18)
- betrayed for thirty pieces of silver (Zech. 11:12–13)

It predicts that

- soldiers would cast lots for his garments (Ps. 22:18, John. 19:23–24)
- his side would be pierced (Zech. 12:10)
- he would be crushed by evil men (Ps. 22:16–18, Zech.12:10)
- he would rise from the dead (Ps. 16:10)

In addition to this sampling of fulfilled prophecy, we have the New Testament record of Jesus Himself predicting His own death and resurrection found in all four Gospels. Beyond the prophecies of His own resurrection, there are sixty-one Old Testament prophecies that Jesus literally fulfilled.

COMPOUND PROBABILITY

Peter Stoner in his book *Science Speaks* discusses the mathematical probability of just eight of those sixty-one prophecies being fulfilled. A word picture helps to understand how difficult this is to do. Imagine filling the state of Texas two feet deep with silver dollars. Paint one red, blindfold someone, and let them go anywhere in Texas and see if they can pick out the red silver dollar on the first try!

How could ordinary men have known these events would come through one person? The only logical explanation is that they would have to have been given this knowledge by someone who knew the future. Fulfilled predictions set the Bible apart from every other religious book. No other book comes close to the Bible's predictive accuracy.

Cyrus

One of the most specific Old Testament predictions identifies Cyrus King of Persia before he was even born. Isaiah prophesies, "I am the LORD…who says of Cyrus, 'He is my shepherd and will accomplish all that I please; he will say of Jerusalem, 'Let it be rebuilt,' and of the temple, 'Let its foundations be laid.' This is what the LORD says to his anointed, to Cyrus, whose right hand I take hold of to subdue nations before him…to open doors before him so that gates will not be shut" (Isaiah 44:24,28, 45:1).

This prediction was made some 150 years before Cyrus was born, since Isaiah lived between 740 and 690 BC, and Cyrus did not make his proclamation for Israel to return from exile until about 536 BC. There would have been no human way for Isaiah to know what Cyrus would be named or do.

Tyre

Tyre was an important seaport in the eastern Mediterranean and one of the great cities of the ancient world.

It was a heavily fortified and flourishing city. Yet Ezekiel 26:3–14 predicted its entire demolition hundreds of years in advance:

> This is what the Sovereign LORD says: I am against you, Tyre, and I will bring many nations against you, like the sea casting up its waves. They will destroy the walls of Tyre and pull down her towers; I will scrape away her rubble and make her a bare rock. Out in the sea she will become a place to spread fishnets, for I have spoken, declares the Sovereign LORD.... They will plunder your wealth and loot your merchandise; they will break down your walls and demolish your fine houses and throw your stones, timber and rubble into the sea.... You will never be rebuilt, for I the LORD have spoken, declares the Sovereign LORD.

This prediction was literally fulfilled by Nebuchadnezzar, who destroyed the city and left it in ruins. However, the stones, dust, and timber were not thrown into the sea. Then Alexander the Great some three hundred years later attacked the seemingly impregnable island of Tyre by taking the stones, dust, and timber from the ruined city and building the causeway to the island. Not only has the city never been rebuilt, but today it literally is used as a "place to spread fishnets."

The issue of predictive prophecy remains, in my mind, the most compelling of all the evidence in favor of the supernatural origin of the Bible. My research has led me to conclude that either a supernatural being who somehow dwells outside of time has somehow predicted the future without violating human free will, or the prophecies and their fulfillment in time came about by an incredibly "lucky" combination of time plus matter plus chance. I have made my choice on where to place my faith. I encourage you to place yours in God and His Word, the Holy Bible.

CHAPTER 7

The "Doink" Heard Round the World (Manuscripts)

"The Dead Sea Scrolls have shown that our traditional Bible has been amazingly, accurately preserved for over 2,000 years."

—Eugene Ulrich, editor of *Oxford's Dead Sea Scrolls Series*

In March 1947, two Arab teenagers were tending their goats and sheep near the ancient settlement of Qumran, located on the northwest shore of the Dead Sea. One of the boys tossed a rock into a cliffside opening, and he was surprised to hear a shattering sound. We could call it the "doink" heard round the world! The accidental discovery of what we call the Dead Sea Scrolls (DSS) has since been dubbed the greatest archaeological find of all time.

The importance of these scrolls cannot be overemphasized. Every Old Testament book except Esther is represented by at least fragments. The entire book of Isaiah was found on one scroll twenty-four feet long. Before 1947 the oldest text of Isaiah was dated at around AD 900, but the DSS copy dated to 100 BC shows that over a period of about one thousand years the text of Isaiah had been preserved with incredible accuracy. It is the oldest biblical scroll in existence.

Bible scholar Gleason Archer observes that the two copies of Isaiah discovered in Qumran Cave 1 "proved to be word-for-word identical with our standard Hebrew Bible in more than 95% of the text, the 5% being obvious slips of the pen and spelling errors."

The importance of this discovery is not just that the DSS manuscripts predate Christ and are in good condition, but that they contain the clearest and most complete prophecy about the coming Messiah.

The caves were occupied into the early Christian era, and some DSS fragments have been identified as the earliest known pieces of the New Testament. In 1972 a Spanish Jesuit archaeologist named José O'Callaghan announced that he had found text from the Gospel of Mark on a DSS fragment, the earliest known piece of Mark in antiquity. Other fragments from Cave 7 contained text believed to be from Acts, Romans, 1 Timothy, 1 Peter, and James. *The New York Times*, United Press International, and *TIME* magazine all reported on O'Callaghan's conclusions, which suggested that the Gospel of Mark was written within the lifetime of the apostles. The fragments identified represent every major section of the New Testament: the Gospels, Acts, and both Pauline and general epistles. All thanks to the Dead Sea Scrolls!

MANUSCRIPT NUMBERS

Since we do not have the original "autographs" (first generation writings), textual critics aim to determine the reliability of existing Bible copies that we do have. For any collection of works, the greater the number and the earlier the dating of the manuscripts, the easier it is to reconstruct a text closer to the original and identify errors or discrepancies.

According to the Center for the Study of New Testament Manuscripts, we have 5,856 Greek manuscripts (either whole or fragments). The non-Greek manuscripts (Armenian, Latin, etc.) account for a total of 23,986. The earliest manuscript we have is dated AD 130.

If we were to compare this to the number of existing manuscripts or fragments of other ancient writings, there is a stark contrast. Homer's *Iliad* and *Odyssey* have 1,757 copies, *Caesar's Gallic Wars* has 10 copies, Tacitus's *Greek History* has 20 copies, and so on.

How do the New Testament documents compare with other ancient books? A stack of existing manuscripts from the average classical writer would measure about four feet high. The New Testament manuscripts would stack to more than one mile high.

CHAPTER 8

Canon Fodder

(How We Know Which Books Belong in the Bible)

"The recognition of God's Word is usually called 'canonization,' and we are careful to say that God determined the canon, and the church discovered the canon. The canon of scripture was not created by the church, rather the church discovered and recognized God's Word as inspired and authoritative since its inception."

—Michael Kruger, *Canon Revisited*

We have a God who has revealed Himself to us! He has revealed Himself in His creation (Ps. 19:1–4, Rom. 1:19–20) and in our consciences (Rom. 2:14–15). He has revealed Himself in Jesus (Heb. 1:3; Col. 1:15, 2:9; John 14:8–9) and through His Holy Spirit (John 16:13–15, 1 Cor. 2:10–12). God has also revealed Himself in Scripture. God has communicated to mankind by means of written script. Hence the term *scripture.* We have access to that revelation in our Bibles.

In Exodus 17:14 we find the first mention of God commanding men to write stuff down as a means of His revealing Himself. As time went on, Moses and other inspired writers—the prophets of the Old Testament and the apostles of the New—added contributions to what we now call the unique biblical *canon,* a word meaning "measuring rod." The canon is a set of books meeting a standard agreed upon by the early church as to be so divinely inspired that we could confidently view them as direct communication from Heaven. These writings would add to what God had already revealed about Himself in His creation and in our consciences.

As time has passed, of course, many other religious books have been written. Some claim to be from God. But questions regarding the Old and New Testaments were settled long ago with regards to the authenticity, trustworthiness, and authority of the books.

Michael Kruger, one of the world's foremost authorities on the subject, explains:

> Many writings by church leaders were in circulation during the two centuries after Christ's ascension. So in AD 170, leaders began to settle the matter by establishing the Muratorian Canon, which declared all Old Testament books, the Four Gospels, and most other New Testament books to be divinely inspired. Later councils added in the books of Hebrews, James, 1 and 2 Peter, and 3 John.[1]

WHY THESE BOOKS?

Contrary to popular myths like *The Da Vinci Code*, the New Testament canon did not suddenly drop out of heaven on golden plates (á la the Book of Mormon or the Koran). Nor did it appear when a few pot-bellied scholars emerged from a smoke-filled room and threw out all the books that didn't meet their standards, finally settling on the twenty-seven New Testament books we now hold so dear. No. There was no vote taken and no political agenda foisted on a naive population.

As Kruger explains in the quotation selected to begin this chapter, the canon of Scripture was not created by the church; rather, the church discovered and recognized the divine stamp of approval upon the sixty-six books of what we now call the Bible.

Kruger defines *canon* as a collection of scriptural books that God has given His people, which are distinguished by their divine qualities, such as their consistent portrait of the character of God and their recognition and use by the early church. Utmost importance was given to their apostolic connection. Most of the New Testament books were composed by one of the apostles, including Paul. Those New Testament writers who were not apostles themselves had close links to the testimony of the apostles, such as Luke, who traveled with Paul. Sound orthodox doctrine was also a determining factor as the content would carry delegated authority from God. An important test was consistency with the already accepted Four Gospels, Matthew, Mark, Luke, and John.

Toward the end of the first century and well into the second, a false movement called Gnosticism crept into the new churches, teaching among other things that all matter is evil and that salvation comes through esoteric knowledge (*gnosis*), a kind of secret mystical knowing opened to only a privileged few. This, of course, was directly opposed to Scripture, which taught that Jesus came in the flesh (John 1:14) and rose again physically (1 Cor. 15:1–22) and that salvation was open to all by personal knowledge of Christ (John 17:3, 1 Cor. 15:1–4).

Two examples of books that didn't "make the cut" were the gnostic Gospels of Peter and Thomas. These books were purported to have been written by the two apostles, but they were easily dismissed because of their questionable content. Judge for yourself:

> Simon Peter said to them: "Let Mary go away from us, for women are not worthy of life." Jesus said, "Look, I will draw her in so as to make her male, so that she too may become a living male spirit similar to you." But I say to you, "Every woman who makes herself male will enter the kingdom of heaven." (Gospel of Thomas, 114)

Similarly, the Gospel of Peter fancies a talking cross that converses with God and features a gigantic Jesus whose head literally ascends into the clouds! (Gospel of Peter 10.39–42)

The canonical books were not "chosen" in some type of canonical contest but were already in circulation from the latter first century on. These books were grouped together by God's people, with the Old Testament canon settled by the birth of Jesus.

Most of the New Testament was written in the first century. Although the twenty-seven books we now recognize as the New Testament were not officially settled upon for three hundred years, at least twenty-two of the books were in wide circulation within the church in the first and second centuries.

So, in summary, how did the church recognize what books "measured up" sufficiently to be recognized as the "God-breathed" (2 Tim. 3:16) inspirational books we now call the Bible? Key to the church's recognition of the canon were the authenticity, trustworthiness, and authority of the books; their consistent portrait of the character of God; their recognition and use by the early church; their apostolic connection; and their sound orthodox doctrine.

Some have suggested there is a chain of attributes through which these books were tested:

1. First by *inspiration* in which God breathes the words that human agents recorded (2 Tim. 3:16).

2. After that came *dissemination*. That is, the Word was delivered to its audience through preaching or other means.

3. There was a *recognition* as God's people distinguished the holy scripture from other writings.

4. Then *preservation* through which God's Word has survived to the present day through the Dead Sea Scrolls and other archaeological, prophetic, and manuscript evidence.

5. Finally, *illumination* as the Holy Spirit opens the believers' understanding so they receive the Word as indeed inspired.

CHAPTER 9

But Does It Work? (Orthodoxy and Orthopraxy)

"For Jesus, as for the psalmist, God's Word was the lamp for his feet and a light for his path. The Bible is not merely a handbook of private piety. It is the very foundation of Western civilization."

—Vishal Mangalwadi, *The Book That Made Your World*

If you have made it this far, I presume that you have at least partially bought into my thesis that indeed the Holy Bible is wholly true. I would also presume that if the Bible is as great as many of us say it is, then it follows logically that we might ask, "Does it work?" Do its claims stand the scrutiny of the skeptic who may ask, "So what?"

What's the difference between the Bible and other religious writings like the Quran, the Bhagavad Gita, or the Book of Mormon, all of which lay claim to truth? What makes the Bible "useful" (see chapter 2) for all practical purposes?

Technically speaking, if the Bible is indeed "wholly true," we should obey it whether it "works" or not, but the Bible declares that "faith without works is dead" (James 2:20 KJV). While pragmatism (assessing the truth of a given theory in terms of its success) is not our means of determining truth, nonetheless orthodoxy (right belief) without orthopraxy (right action) is dead faith.

The apostle John wrote that if we don't obey God's commands and love one another, our orthodoxy is counterfeit (1 John 2:4, 3:15). However, while history shows Bible-toting Christians have their share of hypocrisy, the record also shows that when orthodoxy is believed and obeyed, orthopraxy is soon to follow.

Orthodoxy and *orthopraxy* are compound Greek words. The first word in both compounds is *ortho,* which is quite familiar to most of us today. It means "right, correct, or straight." An orthodontist is a dentist who can straighten or correct teeth. An orthopedist is a doctor who works with deformities or misalignments of the skeletal system, often the spine, with the hope of being able to correct them. *Doxy* is Greek for belief. *Praxis* sounds like its English equivalent—*practice.* So orthodoxy is right, or correct, belief, and orthopraxy or orthopraxis is simply "correct practice" or "correct behavior."

I have numerous history books that document examples of transformed individuals and nations. The following are just a sampling of the positive changes that happen when God's people combine orthodoxy and orthopraxy:

- Along with many fellow evangelical leaders, American evangelist and abolitionist Charles Finney preached against slavery and worked for abolition as well as education for women and blacks.
- Motivated by his Christian faith, British politician William Wilberforce worked tirelessly to end the transatlantic slave trade between Africa, Great Britain, and the Americas and advocated for the complete abolition of slavery.
- Many historians credit the preaching of John Wesley for saving England from a bloody revolution like the one that terrorized France just a few years before.
- The emergence of the modern university came from biblical revelation of a trinitarian divinity who was one God (unity) in three persons (diversity).
- First US President George Washington did not want to be a king because he had a biblical worldview (remember *Weltanschauung*?) that included an understanding of original sin and the need for accountability in government. Hence the framers of the Constitution cited Isaiah 33:22, where God's character is described as a Judge, Lawgiver, and King. This evolved into the judicial, legislative, and executive

branches of the US government, which provide separation of powers and checks and balances designed to prevent the kind of tyranny American colonists experienced under King George.

- Vishal Mangalwadi's epic tome *The Book That Made Your World: How the Bible Created the Soul of Western Civilization* chronicles how the Bible's influence is responsible for much of the social progress in the Western world.
- The late sociologist of religion and longtime Baylor University professor Rodney Stark published the results of a ten-year peer-reviewed study on the effects of Bible-believing missionaries around the world. His findings: "By introducing religious liberty, mass education, mass printing, newspapers, literacy, care for the poor, the unborn, the oppressed, widows, orphans and other marginalized peoples, many were liberated, and societies were transformed."[1] One great example Stark cites is William Carey, who lobbied to end the horrible practice of *suttee* (widow-burning) in India.

Many more illustrations could be given of nations, tribes, families, and language groups that have been radically saved by a supernatural God and His supernatural Book.

I myself was converted during the Jesus Movement, in which thousands of young people like me were delivered from drugs, alcohol, and other false comforts when we submitted our lives to the God who brings lasting comfort to the soul. I was sitting on a California beach when two young surfers approached me with a gospel booklet containing Bible verses about how I could be "saved." That word went straight to my heart.

Many of these "Jesus People" planted Bible-believing churches around the world. Pastor Chuck Smith, who has been called the father of the Jesus Movement, credits "simply teaching the Bible simply" as a central element in the revival. Below are short stories of some of my friends whose lives were radically transformed by the power of God's Word:

- My friend Mike MacIntosh was diagnosed with paranoid schizophrenia at the Orange County Medical Center because of too many bad "acid trips" (LSD) and wandered into Pastor Chuck's church. He was converted under the preaching of another friend, hippie evangelist Lonnie Frisbee, who went on to win hundreds to Christ after undergoing a miraculous conversion to Christ in the Southern California desert.
- Another friend, Raul Ries, was sent home from Vietnam because he threatened to kill his commanding officer. Later, while contemplating killing his wife and himself, he was dramatically converted when he heard Chuck preaching the gospel on television. Raul went on to plant

many churches and has a powerful ministry in the Latin world.

- Another friend, Rabi Maharaj, was a Hindu guru who was converted. Today he is an effective evangelist.
- Nicky Cruz, a vicious streetfighter and gang member on the streets of New York, was led to faith in Jesus by David Wilkerson. His story is told in the best-selling book *The Cross and the Switchblade*.

I could go on. Where the Bible is believed and obeyed, God's supernatural power is displayed.

Does the Bible work? You bet it does!

APPENDIX

The Word to the World

(Ending Bible Poverty)

"Now there were staying in Jerusalem God-fearing Jews from every nation under heaven. When they heard this sound, a crowd came together in bewilderment, because each one heard their own language being spoken. Utterly amazed, they asked: ...'How is it that each of us hears them in our native language?... We hear them declaring the wonders of God in our own tongues!'"—Acts 2:5–11

"After this I looked, and there before me was a great multitude that no one could count, from every nation, tribe, people and language, standing before the throne and before the Lamb."—Revelation 7:9

"The greatest missionary in the world is the Bible in the mother tongue. It needs no furlough and is never considered a foreigner.... Understanding Scripture in a language other than the heart language is like trying to eat soup with a fork. You can get a little taste, but you cannot get nourished."

—Cameron Townsend,
Founder, Wycliffe Bible Translators

"If your God is so great, why doesn't He speak our language?"

—a Cakchiquel native
to Bible translator Cameron Townsend

According to Wycliffe Global Alliance, as of 2024, there were 756 languages with translations of the complete Bible and 1,726 more languages with just New Testament translations. This sounds like a bunch, and it is, until we factor in that there are 773 million illiterate adults and millions more who can read the trade language but still have no translations in their mother tongue, or heart language.

A few years ago, a veteran linguist calculated that at the present rate it would take 150 years to make heart-language translations available to the last Bibleless group. Then some creative minds started churning with a passion to speed things up. Hence Oral Bible Translation (OBT) was born.

"Oral Bible Translation is a mother-tongue, speaker-centered approach to Bible translation in which both translation and quality assurance processes are trustworthy and appropriate, carried out mostly orally, with the end result being an oral Scripture that is trustworthy, appropriate, intelligible, and appealing," said Brazilian linguist Marcia Suzuki.

OBT is not just an audio recording of literacy-based methods and tools, but an approach that seeks to record an internalized Bible passage by heart by someone from the host culture. It goes something like this:

- Some people from a Bibleless group express a desire to orally translate a book of the Bible in their mother tongue.
- A small team is formed from a mission agency or church and teams up with prospective translators to support them.
- The team is trained in how to facilitate an oral translation and in how to train the translators. This way people from the community can have active roles in the translation and can exert leadership in the project whether or not they can read or write.
- Facilitators also learn to operate orally so that their participation does not disrupt the oral dynamics of the translation process.
- The recorded draft is checked for quality assurance by other translators and by members of the community, mentors, and/or consultants.
- The translation team receives feedback and continues to improve their oral draft.
- The process is repeated until the translation receives the approval of all involved parties.
- The approved translation is recorded and officially authenticated by the appropriate

group, be it a local church, mission agency, or community.

- The recording is produced and is now regarded as the authoritative oral translation of that passage of Scripture in that language and for distribution to the community for their engagement with the Word of God.

Verbal recordings of the Bible are more than a stopgap or temporary measure. They are giving the Word of God to people who otherwise would have no access to God's Word simply because they are illiterate.

The work of Bible translators and linguists will always be needed. They have been at the forefront of Bible-translation work for hundreds of years. They do a painstaking labor of love, taking years to learn a new language in a field with no one to teach them, identifying the grammar of that language, and sometimes devising written symbols.

We need both: those doing verbally recorded Bibles and highly trained linguists who produce written copies of God's Word in the languages of the people. When missionaries give their verbally recorded Bibles to translators, it helps the linguists produce quality written translations much sooner. How wonderful to shorten the wait for written Bibles by years!

The overall work of getting the Bible to every people group is speeding up. Missionaries are quickly creating verbal Bibles in new languages for hundreds of millions who can't read. People are downloading verbal Bibles from the Internet and sharing them with one another on micro-SD cards. They import Scriptures in their language into their mobile phones and handheld devices. This is a huge boost in places like Papua New Guinea, where there are 1,121 languages, 426 of which lack any portion of the Bible.

Robin Green of Faith Comes by Hearing developed an app in partnership with Pioneer Bible translators and the Seed Company. It's called Render. They designed it so that illiterate people can make verbal recordings of the Bible for their tribe.

A local interpreter listens to the Bible in the majority language of his or her country and then creates a verbal recording in the mother tongue. Verbal recordings save local interpreters the work of learning to read, then creating an alphabet, teaching literacy to the community, and writing down the translated Bible. It also saves an outsider from having to learn a new language, study its grammar, and create written symbols—all before they can begin translation! If they begin instead with verbal recordings, they can offer the people recorded Bibles quickly.

I humbly submit that it is unjust for one language—English—to have more than one hundred complete translations while hundreds of people groups have none. This is the time for us to end Bible poverty and to work and pray hard to let the Earth hear His voice!

ENDNOTES

Introduction

1. Clarence Hall, "Shimabuku: The Village that Lives by the Bible," *Reader's Digest*, January 1961.

Chapter 1

Epigraph—John R. W. Stott, *I Believe in Preaching* (Hodder Christian Books, 1993).

1. The Word introduction, *Christian Growth Study Bible* (Zondervan Publishing, 1997), 637.
2. Lee Strobel, *The Case for Faith: A Journalist Investigates the Toughest Objections to Christianity* (Zondervan, 2021).

Chapter 2

Epigraph—Eugene Peterson, *Eat This Book: A Conversation in the Art of Spiritual Reading* (Eerdmans, 2006).

Chapter 3

Epigraph—Richard Bauckham, *Jesus and the Eyewitnesses: The Gospels as Eyewitness Testimony* (Eerdmans, 2006), 7.

Chapter 4

Epigraph—David Noebel, *The Battle for Truth* (Harvest House: 2001).

1. Darlene Cunningham, *Values Matter: Stories of the Beliefs and Values That Shaped Youth With A Mission* (YWAM Publishing, 2020), 37.
2. John Stott, *Christian Mission in the Modern World* (IVP, 2008).

Chapter 5

Epigraph—Nelson Glueck, *Rivers in the Desert: A History of the Negev* (Farrar, Straus and Cudahy, 1959), 31.

1. Hank Hanegraaff, "The Bible: Human or Divine?" (Bible Answer Man, 2010).

Chapter 6

Epigraph—Thomas D. Ice, "The Literal Fulfillment of Bible Prophecy" (2009). *Article Archives.* 101. https://digitalcommons.liberty.edu/pretrib_arch/101/)

Chapter 7

Epigraph—Eugene Ulrich, qtd. by Jeffery L. Sheler in *Is the Bible True? How Modern Debates and Discoveries Affirm the Essence of the Scriptures* (Zondervan, 1999), 151.

Chapter 8

Epigraph—Michael Kruger, *Canon Revisited: Establishing the Origins and Authority of the New Testament Books* (Crossway, 2012).

1. Michael Kruger, *The Question of Canon: Challenging the status quo in the New Testament debate* (IVP, 2020).

Chapter 9

Epigraph—Vishal Mangalwadi, *The Book That Made Your World: How the Bible Created the Soul of Western Civilization* (Thomas Nelson, 2012).

1. Rodney Stark, *The Rise of Christianity: How the Obscure, Marginal Jesus Movement Became the Dominant Religious Force in the Western World in a Few Centuries* (Princeton University Press, 1996).

ABOUT THE AUTHOR

Danny Lehmann is the Dean of the College of Christian Ministries for the University of the Nations. He joined Youth With a Mission in 1980 and was formerly the campus director at YWAM Honolulu. He also served on YWAM's Global Leadership Team. Danny travels internationally to teach on evangelism, missions, and discipleship. He lives in Kailua-Kona, Hawaii, with his wife, Linda. He has two sons, Daniel and David, and seven grandchildren.

OTHER RESOURCES BY DANNY LEHMANN

- Is there such a thing as "Truth" and can we know it?
- Does God exist and which God is the "right" God?
- Is the Bible God's Word?
- Did Jesus rise from the dead?
- Can we know where we came from, why we are here, how we should live, and where we are going?

Drawing from more than forty-five years of evangelism experience, Danny Lehmann presents complex issues with simplicity and depth. This book will equip you to know the Truth and be zealous to pass it on to others.

Evangelism. Witnessing. Missions. If these words strike fear in your heart, then this book is for you. Through practical illustrations, personal examples, and clear Bible teaching, Danny examines the messengers, the message, the motives, and the methods of evangelism. *Beautiful Feet* will help you to develop a lifestyle of evangelism.

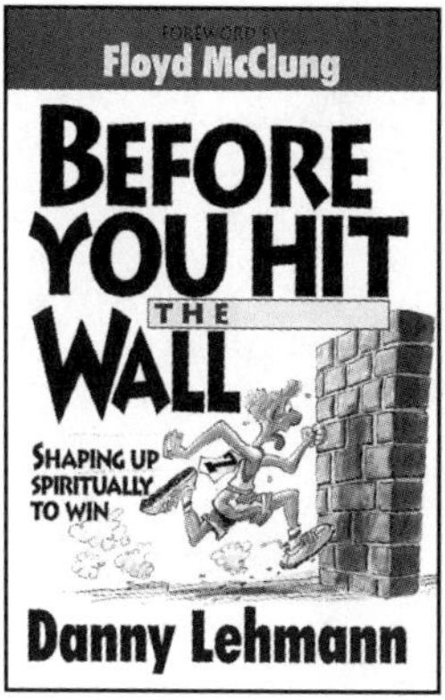

Before You Hit the Wall: Shaping Up Spiritually to Win is Danny Lehmann's current bestselling book. "The Wall" is that formidable obstacle that confronts marathon runners about halfway through a race when they "run out of gas" and decide whether to drop out or press on to the finish. In the spiritual race, we face "The Wall" as well, through trials, testings, and temptations. Will we give up and quit the race, or will we press on to God's destiny for our lives? The answer lies in whether or not we, like marathon runners, have trained our souls through spiritual discipline. This book will help you discover practical ways to make the disciplined life not only attainable, but enjoyable.

Are you stoked for Jesus? If you want the fire of God to burn in your soul, this book is for you! It's all about passion for God. In a time when religious compromise and half-hearted Christianity are more often the rule than the exception, Danny Lehmann teaches you how to rekindle a fiery passion for God and keep the fires stoked for years to come.

Stoked uses powerful illustrations from Scripture, personal insights, and stories from some of the most "stoked" Christians in history to draw readers closer to the heart of God. But beware. If you take its principles to heart, there's no way to avoid being set aflame by the all-consuming love of God.

Little choices can make a big impact. It has been said that the flap of a butterfly's wings in Brazil could ultimately produce a tornado in Texas. Using illustrations like this from nature, society, and the Bible, Danny Lehmann demonstrates that little choices to obey the next thing God puts in front of you, whether big or little in your eyes, can change and make history. However, there is a catch—our definition of big and little must conform to God's. This book will show you how.

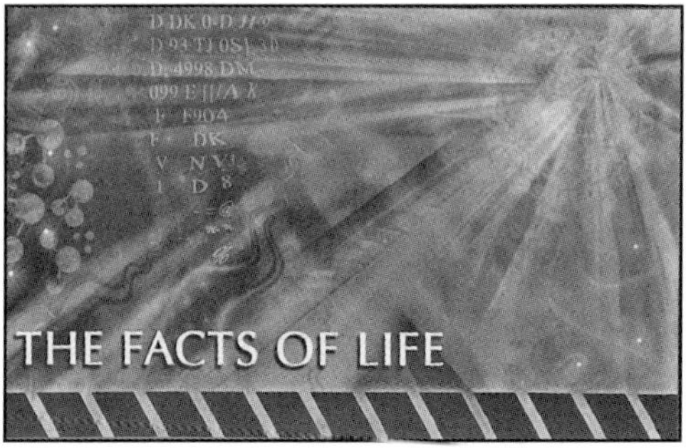

The Facts of Life is an evangelistic tract that goes through four facts and how to receive Christ in a simple format:

1. God loves you and desires that you fulfill the destiny for which you were created.
2. We are separated from God because of our sins.
3. The penalty for our sins is death.
4. Jesus Christ died, and rose again to save us from the power and penalty of sin.

What must I do? 1. Trust, 2. Turn, 3. Follow

The Facts of Life tract is presented on the pages that follow.

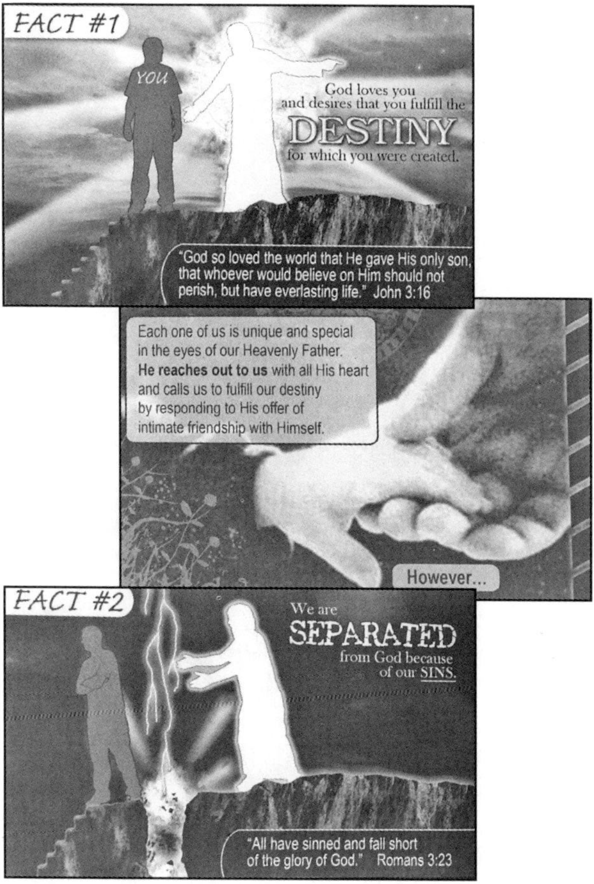
FACT #1
YOU
God loves you
and desires that you fulfill the
DESTINY
for which you were created.
"God so loved the world that He gave His only son, that whoever would believe on Him should not perish, but have everlasting life." John 3:16
Each one of us is unique and special in the eyes of our Heavenly Father. **He reaches out to us** with all His heart and calls us to fulfill our destiny by responding to His offer of intimate friendship with Himself.
However...
FACT #2
We are
SEPARATED
from God because
of our SINS.
"All have sinned and fall short of the glory of God." Romans 3:23

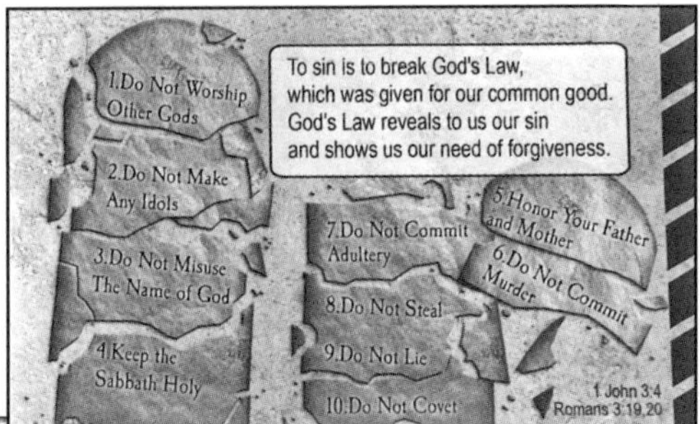
1.Do Not Worship Other Gods
2.Do Not Make Any Idols
3.Do Not Misuse The Name of God
4.Keep the Sabbath Holy
5.Honor Your Father and Mother
6.Do Not Commit Murder
7.Do Not Commit Adultery
8.Do Not Steal
9.Do Not Lie
10.Do Not Covet
To sin is to break God's Law,
which was given for our common good.
God's Law reveals to us our sin
and shows us our need of forgiveness.
1 John 3:4
Romans 3:19,20

FACT #3
The penalty for our sins is
DEATH
"Death passed upon all men
because all haved sinned."
Romans 5:12

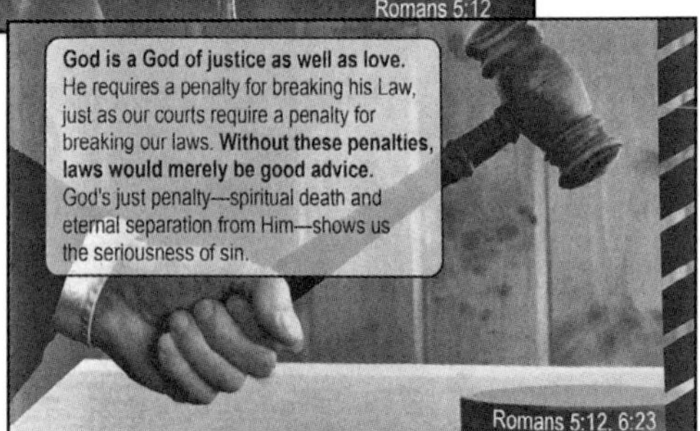
God is a God of justice as well as love.
He requires a penalty for breaking his Law,
just as our courts require a penalty for
breaking our laws. Without these penalties,
laws would merely be good advice.
God's just penalty—spiritual death and
eternal separation from Him—shows us
the seriousness of sin.
Romans 5:12, 6:23

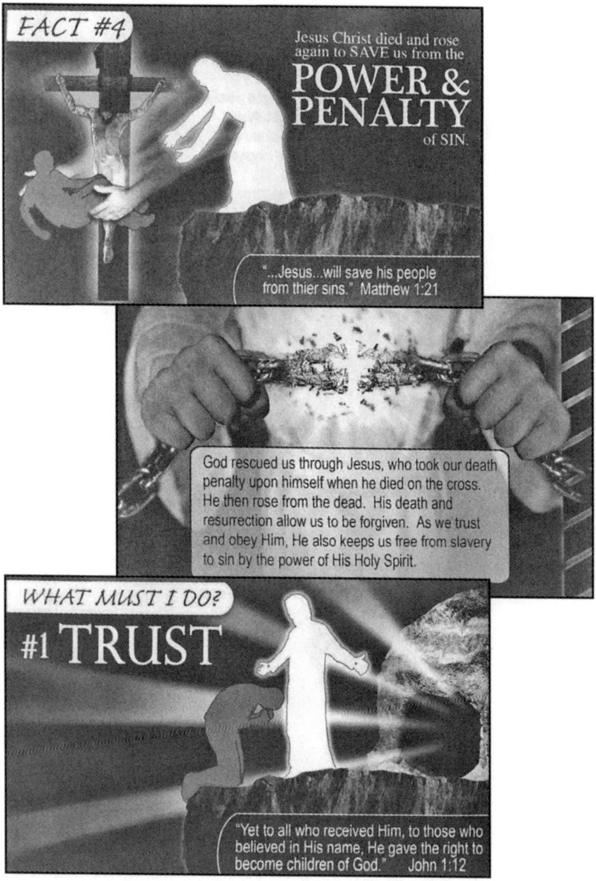
FACT #4
Jesus Christ died and rose again to SAVE us from the
POWER & PENALTY
of SIN.
"...Jesus...will save his people from thier sins." Matthew 1:21
God rescued us through Jesus, who took our death penalty upon himself when he died on the cross. He then rose from the dead. His death and resurrection allow us to be forgiven. As we trust and obey Him, He also keeps us free from slavery to sin by the power of His Holy Spirit.
WHAT MUST I DO?
#1 TRUST
"Yet to all who received Him, to those who believed in His name, He gave the right to become children of God." John 1:12

You must personally receive Jesus by placing your faith in His death and resurrection. To have faith means "to be persuaded." Allow the love of God that was demonstrated for you on the cross persuade you to believe. God's plan is not to threaten you into submission, nor is it to bribe you with the benefits of salvation. He simply wants you to believe His truth and trust Him to save you.
John 1:12
1 Corinthians 15:1-4
WHAT MUST I DO?
#2 TURN
"The kingdom of God is near. Repent and believe the good news!" Mark 1:15
Make the choice to turn away from all known sin. This is called "repentance." To repent is to **change your mind and attitude** towards God and sin. It's like walking down the street one way and Jesus is going the other. He calls you to change your direction, to turn and follow Him. Once you hear His call, you must choose to stop living a sinful and selfish life. God promises His grace to help you.
Acts 3:19,
Acts 20:21
2 Peter 3:9

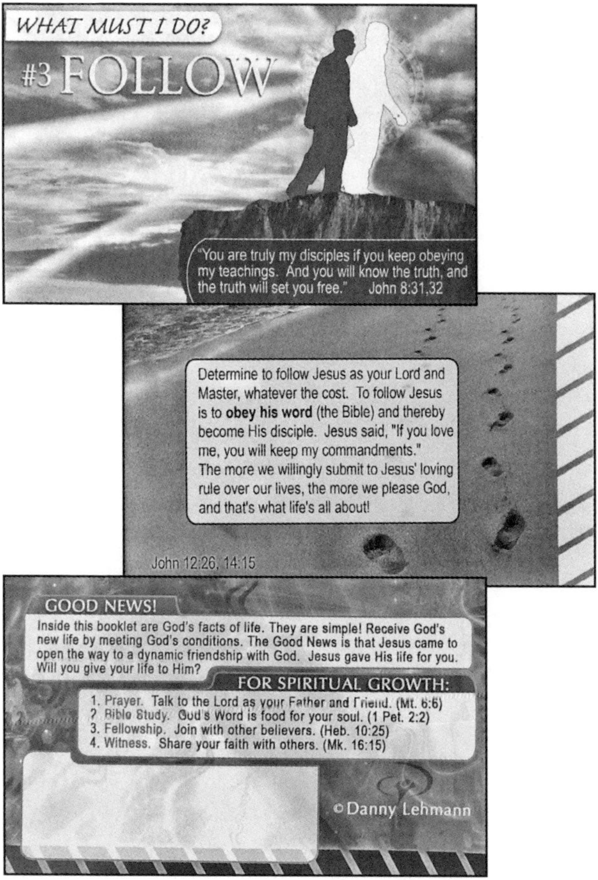
WHAT MUST I DO?
#3 FOLLOW
"You are truly my disciples if you keep obeying my teachings. And you will know the truth, and the truth will set you free." John 8:31,32
Determine to follow Jesus as your Lord and Master, whatever the cost. To follow Jesus is to obey his word (the Bible) and thereby become His disciple. Jesus said, "If you love me, you will keep my commandments." The more we willingly submit to Jesus' loving rule over our lives, the more we please God, and that's what life's all about!
John 12:26, 14:15
GOOD NEWS!
Inside this booklet are God's facts of life. They are simple! Receive God's new life by meeting God's conditions. The Good News is that Jesus came to open the way to a dynamic friendship with God. Jesus gave His life for you. Will you give your life to Him?
FOR SPIRITUAL GROWTH:
1. Prayer. Talk to the Lord as your Father and Friend. (Mt. 6:6)
2. Bible Study. God's Word is food for your soul. (1 Pet. 2:2)
3. Fellowship. Join with other believers. (Heb. 10:25)
4. Witness. Share your faith with others. (Mk. 16:15)
©Danny Lehmann